# STUDY PLANNER

| MOOD ☺ 😄 😐 🙁 😣 | DATE. | | | MON | TUE | WED | THU | FRI | SAT | SUN |
|---|---|---|---|---|---|---|---|---|---|---|

**TODAY'S PRIORITY**

○

○

○

| PLAN | | ○ |
|---|---|---|
| | | ○ |
| | | ○ |
| | | ○ |
| | | ○ |
| | | ○ |
| | | ○ |
| | | ○ |
| | | ○ |
| | | ○ |
| | | ○ |
| | | ○ |
| | | ○ |
| | | ○ |
| | | ○ |
| | | ○ |
| | | ○ |
| | | ○ |
| | | ○ |
| | | ○ |
| | | ○ |

| TOTAL TIME | H | M |
|---|---|---|
| 6 | | |
| 7 | | |
| 8 | | |
| 9 | | |
| 10 | | |
| 11 | | |
| 12 | | |
| 1 | | |
| 2 | | |
| 3 | | |
| 4 | | |
| 5 | | |
| 6 | | |
| 7 | | |
| 8 | | |
| 9 | | |
| 10 | | |
| 11 | | |
| 12 | | |
| 1 | | |
| 2 | | |
| 3 | | |
| 4 | | |
| 5 | | |

**COMMENT**

# STUDY PLANNER

 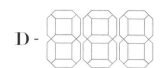

| MOOD ☺☺☺☹☹ | DATE. | MON | TUE | WED | THU | FRI | SAT | SUN |
|---|---|---|---|---|---|---|---|---|

**TODAY'S PRIORITY**

- ○
- ○
- ○

| PLAN | | TOTAL TIME | H | M |
|---|---|---|---|---|
| | ○ | | | |
| | ○ | 6 | | |
| | ○ | 7 | | |
| | ○ | 8 | | |
| | ○ | 9 | | |
| | ○ | 10 | | |
| | ○ | 11 | | |
| | ○ | 12 | | |
| | ○ | 1 | | |
| | ○ | 2 | | |
| | ○ | 3 | | |
| | ○ | 4 | | |
| | ○ | 5 | | |
| | ○ | 6 | | |
| | ○ | 7 | | |
| | ○ | 8 | | |
| | ○ | 9 | | |
| | ○ | 10 | | |
| | ○ | 11 | | |
| | | 12 | | |
| | | 1 | | |
| | | 2 | | |
| | | 3 | | |
| | | 4 | | |
| | | 5 | | |

**COMMENT**

# STUDY PLANNER

 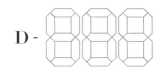

| MOOD ☺ 😊 😐 🙁 😣 | DATE. | MON | TUE | WED | THU | FRI | SAT | SUN |
|---|---|---|---|---|---|---|---|---|

**TODAY'S PRIORITY**

○

○

○

| PLAN | | ○ |
|---|---|---|
| | | ○ |
| | | ○ |
| | | ○ |
| | | ○ |
| | | ○ |
| | | ○ |
| | | ○ |
| | | ○ |
| | | ○ |
| | | ○ |
| | | ○ |
| | | ○ |
| | | ○ |
| | | ○ |
| | | ○ |
| | | ○ |
| | | ○ |
| | | ○ |
| | | ○ |
| | | ○ |

| TOTAL TIME | H | M |
|---|---|---|
| 6 | | |
| 7 | | |
| 8 | | |
| 9 | | |
| 10 | | |
| 11 | | |
| 12 | | |
| 1 | | |
| 2 | | |
| 3 | | |
| 4 | | |
| 5 | | |
| 6 | | |
| 7 | | |
| 8 | | |
| 9 | | |
| 10 | | |
| 11 | | |
| 12 | | |
| 1 | | |
| 2 | | |
| 3 | | |
| 4 | | |
| 5 | | |

COMMENT

# STUDY PLANNER

D -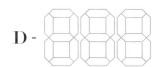

| MOOD ☺ ☻ ☹ ☹ ☹ | DATE. | MON | TUE | WED | THU | FRI | SAT | SUN |
|---|---|---|---|---|---|---|---|---|

**TODAY'S PRIORITY**

○

○

○

| PLAN | | |
|---|---|---|
| | | ○ |
| | | ○ |
| | | ○ |
| | | ○ |
| | | ○ |
| | | ○ |
| | | ○ |
| | | ○ |
| | | ○ |
| | | ○ |
| | | ○ |
| | | ○ |
| | | ○ |
| | | ○ |
| | | ○ |
| | | ○ |
| | | ○ |
| | | ○ |
| | | ○ |
| | | ○ |

| TOTAL TIME | H | M |
|---|---|---|
| 6 | | |
| 7 | | |
| 8 | | |
| 9 | | |
| 10 | | |
| 11 | | |
| 12 | | |
| 1 | | |
| 2 | | |
| 3 | | |
| 4 | | |
| 5 | | |
| 6 | | |
| 7 | | |
| 8 | | |
| 9 | | |
| 10 | | |
| 11 | | |
| 12 | | |
| 1 | | |
| 2 | | |
| 3 | | |
| 4 | | |
| 5 | | |

**COMMENT**

# STUDY PLANNER

D -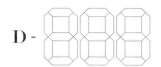

| MOOD ☺ 😄 😐 🙁 😫 | DATE. | | MON | TUE | WED | THU | FRI | SAT | SUN |
|---|---|---|---|---|---|---|---|---|---|

**TODAY'S PRIORITY**

○

○

○

| PLAN | | ○ |
|---|---|---|
| | | ○ |
| | | ○ |
| | | ○ |
| | | ○ |
| | | ○ |
| | | ○ |
| | | ○ |
| | | ○ |
| | | ○ |
| | | ○ |
| | | ○ |
| | | ○ |
| | | ○ |
| | | ○ |
| | | ○ |
| | | ○ |
| | | ○ |
| | | ○ |
| | | ○ |
| | | ○ |
| | | ○ |

| TOTAL TIME | H | M |
|---|---|---|
| 6 | | |
| 7 | | |
| 8 | | |
| 9 | | |
| 10 | | |
| 11 | | |
| 12 | | |
| 1 | | |
| 2 | | |
| 3 | | |
| 4 | | |
| 5 | | |
| 6 | | |
| 7 | | |
| 8 | | |
| 9 | | |
| 10 | | |
| 11 | | |
| 12 | | |
| 1 | | |
| 2 | | |
| 3 | | |
| 4 | | |
| 5 | | |

COMMENT

# STUDY PLANNER

| MOOD ☺ 😊 😐 ☹ 😫 | DATE. | MON | TUE | WED | THU | FRI | SAT | SUN |
|---|---|---|---|---|---|---|---|---|

**TODAY'S PRIORITY**

- ○
- ○
- ○

| PLAN | | | TOTAL TIME | H | M |
|---|---|---|---|---|---|
| | | ○ | | | |
| | | ○ | 6 | | |
| | | ○ | 7 | | |
| | | ○ | 8 | | |
| | | ○ | 9 | | |
| | | ○ | 10 | | |
| | | ○ | 11 | | |
| | | ○ | 12 | | |
| | | ○ | 1 | | |
| | | ○ | 2 | | |
| | | ○ | 3 | | |
| | | ○ | 4 | | |
| | | ○ | 5 | | |
| | | ○ | 6 | | |
| | | ○ | 7 | | |
| | | ○ | 8 | | |
| | | ○ | 9 | | |
| | | ○ | 10 | | |
| | | ○ | 11 | | |
| | | | 12 | | |
| | | | 1 | | |
| | | | 2 | | |
| | | | 3 | | |
| | | | 4 | | |
| | | | 5 | | |

**COMMENT**

# STUDY PLANNER

D -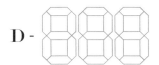

| MOOD ☺ ☺ ☺ ☹ ☹ | DATE. | MON | TUE | WED | THU | FRI | SAT | SUN |
|---|---|---|---|---|---|---|---|---|

**TODAY'S PRIORITY**

- ○
- ○
- ○

| PLAN | | |
|---|---|---|
| | | ○ |
| | | ○ |
| | | ○ |
| | | ○ |
| | | ○ |
| | | ○ |
| | | ○ |
| | | ○ |
| | | ○ |
| | | ○ |
| | | ○ |
| | | ○ |
| | | ○ |
| | | ○ |
| | | ○ |
| | | ○ |
| | | ○ |
| | | ○ |
| | | ○ |
| | | ○ |
| | | ○ |
| | | ○ |

| TOTAL TIME | H | M |
|---|---|---|
| 6 | | |
| 7 | | |
| 8 | | |
| 9 | | |
| 10 | | |
| 11 | | |
| 12 | | |
| 1 | | |
| 2 | | |
| 3 | | |
| 4 | | |
| 5 | | |
| 6 | | |
| 7 | | |
| 8 | | |
| 9 | | |
| 10 | | |
| 11 | | |
| 12 | | |
| 1 | | |
| 2 | | |
| 3 | | |
| 4 | | |
| 5 | | |

**COMMENT**

# STUDY PLANNER

D -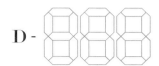

| MOOD ☺ 😊 😐 🙁 😣 | DATE. | | MON | TUE | WED | THU | FRI | SAT | SUN |
|---|---|---|---|---|---|---|---|---|---|

**TODAY'S PRIORITY**

- ○
- ○
- ○

| PLAN | | ○ |
|---|---|---|
| | | ○ |
| | | ○ |
| | | ○ |
| | | ○ |
| | | ○ |
| | | ○ |
| | | ○ |
| | | ○ |
| | | ○ |
| | | ○ |
| | | ○ |
| | | ○ |
| | | ○ |
| | | ○ |
| | | ○ |
| | | ○ |
| | | ○ |
| | | ○ |
| | | ○ |
| | | ○ |

| TOTAL TIME | H | M |
|---|---|---|
| 6 | | |
| 7 | | |
| 8 | | |
| 9 | | |
| 10 | | |
| 11 | | |
| 12 | | |
| 1 | | |
| 2 | | |
| 3 | | |
| 4 | | |
| 5 | | |
| 6 | | |
| 7 | | |
| 8 | | |
| 9 | | |
| 10 | | |
| 11 | | |
| 12 | | |
| 1 | | |
| 2 | | |
| 3 | | |
| 4 | | |
| 5 | | |

**COMMENT**

# STUDY PLANNER

D -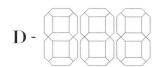

| MOOD ☺ 😊 😐 🙁 😣 | DATE. | | MON | TUE | WED | THU | FRI | SAT | SUN |
|---|---|---|---|---|---|---|---|---|---|

**TODAY'S PRIORITY**

- ○
- ○
- ○

| PLAN | | | TOTAL TIME | H | M |
|---|---|---|---|---|---|
| | ○ | | 6 | | |
| | ○ | | 7 | | |
| | ○ | | 8 | | |
| | ○ | | 9 | | |
| | ○ | | 10 | | |
| | ○ | | 11 | | |
| | ○ | | 12 | | |
| | ○ | | 1 | | |
| | ○ | | 2 | | |
| | ○ | | 3 | | |
| | ○ | | 4 | | |
| | ○ | | 5 | | |
| | ○ | | 6 | | |
| | ○ | | 7 | | |
| | ○ | | 8 | | |
| | ○ | | 9 | | |
| | ○ | | 10 | | |
| | ○ | | 11 | | |
| | | | 12 | | |
| | | | 1 | | |
| | | | 2 | | |
| | | | 3 | | |
| | | | 4 | | |
| | | | 5 | | |

**COMMENT**

# STUDY PLANNER

 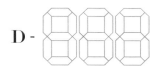

| MOOD ☺ 😄 😐 🙁 😣 | DATE. | MON | TUE | WED | THU | FRI | SAT | SUN |
|---|---|---|---|---|---|---|---|---|

**TODAY'S PRIORITY**

- ○
- ○
- ○

| PLAN | | | TOTAL TIME | H | M |
|---|---|---|---|---|---|
| | | ○ | 6 | | |
| | | ○ | 7 | | |
| | | ○ | 8 | | |
| | | ○ | 9 | | |
| | | ○ | 10 | | |
| | | ○ | 11 | | |
| | | ○ | 12 | | |
| | | ○ | 1 | | |
| | | ○ | 2 | | |
| | | ○ | 3 | | |
| | | ○ | 4 | | |
| | | ○ | 5 | | |
| | | ○ | 6 | | |
| | | ○ | 7 | | |
| | | ○ | 8 | | |
| | | ○ | 9 | | |
| | | ○ | 10 | | |
| | | ○ | 11 | | |
| | | | 12 | | |
| | | | 1 | | |
| | | | 2 | | |
| | | | 3 | | |
| | | | 4 | | |
| | | | 5 | | |

**COMMENT**

# STUDY PLANNER

 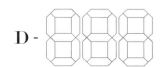

| MOOD ☺ 😀 😐 🙁 😣 | DATE. | | MON | TUE | WED | THU | FRI | SAT | SUN |
|---|---|---|---|---|---|---|---|---|---|

**TODAY'S PRIORITY**

○

○

○

| PLAN | | ○ |
|---|---|---|
| | | ○ |
| | | ○ |
| | | ○ |
| | | ○ |
| | | ○ |
| | | ○ |
| | | ○ |
| | | ○ |
| | | ○ |
| | | ○ |
| | | ○ |
| | | ○ |
| | | ○ |
| | | ○ |
| | | ○ |
| | | ○ |
| | | ○ |
| | | ○ |
| | | ○ |

| TOTAL TIME | H | M |
|---|---|---|
| 6 | | |
| 7 | | |
| 8 | | |
| 9 | | |
| 10 | | |
| 11 | | |
| 12 | | |
| 1 | | |
| 2 | | |
| 3 | | |
| 4 | | |
| 5 | | |
| 6 | | |
| 7 | | |
| 8 | | |
| 9 | | |
| 10 | | |
| 11 | | |
| 12 | | |
| 1 | | |
| 2 | | |
| 3 | | |
| 4 | | |
| 5 | | |

**COMMENT**

# STUDY PLANNER

 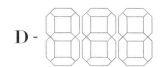

| MOOD ☺ ☺ ☺ ☹ ☹ | DATE. | MON | TUE | WED | THU | FRI | SAT | SUN |
|---|---|---|---|---|---|---|---|---|

**TODAY'S PRIORITY**

○

○

○

| PLAN | | ○ |
|---|---|---|
| | | ○ |
| | | ○ |
| | | ○ |
| | | ○ |
| | | ○ |
| | | ○ |
| | | ○ |
| | | ○ |
| | | ○ |
| | | ○ |
| | | ○ |
| | | ○ |
| | | ○ |
| | | ○ |
| | | ○ |
| | | ○ |
| | | ○ |
| | | ○ |
| | | ○ |
| | | ○ |
| | | ○ |

| TOTAL TIME | H | M |
|---|---|---|
| 6 | | |
| 7 | | |
| 8 | | |
| 9 | | |
| 10 | | |
| 11 | | |
| 12 | | |
| 1 | | |
| 2 | | |
| 3 | | |
| 4 | | |
| 5 | | |
| 6 | | |
| 7 | | |
| 8 | | |
| 9 | | |
| 10 | | |
| 11 | | |
| 12 | | |
| 1 | | |
| 2 | | |
| 3 | | |
| 4 | | |
| 5 | | |

**COMMENT**

# STUDY PLANNER

 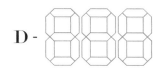

| MOOD ☺ ☺ ☺ ☹ ☹ | DATE. | MON | TUE | WED | THU | FRI | SAT | SUN |
|---|---|---|---|---|---|---|---|---|

**TODAY'S PRIORITY**

- ○
- ○
- ○

| PLAN | | | TOTAL TIME | H | M |
|---|---|---|---|---|---|
| | | ○ | 6 | | |
| | | ○ | 7 | | |
| | | ○ | 8 | | |
| | | ○ | 9 | | |
| | | ○ | 10 | | |
| | | ○ | 11 | | |
| | | ○ | 12 | | |
| | | ○ | 1 | | |
| | | ○ | 2 | | |
| | | ○ | 3 | | |
| | | ○ | 4 | | |
| | | ○ | 5 | | |
| | | ○ | 6 | | |
| | | ○ | 7 | | |
| | | ○ | 8 | | |
| | | ○ | 9 | | |
| | | ○ | 10 | | |
| | | ○ | 11 | | |
| | | | 12 | | |
| | | | 1 | | |
| | | | 2 | | |
| | | | 3 | | |
| | | | 4 | | |
| | | | 5 | | |

**COMMENT**

# STUDY PLANNER

D -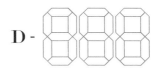

| MOOD ☺ ☺ ☺ ☹ ☹ | DATE. | | MON | TUE | WED | THU | FRI | SAT | SUN |
|---|---|---|---|---|---|---|---|---|---|

**TODAY'S PRIORITY**

○

○

○

| PLAN | | ○ |
|---|---|---|
| | | ○ |
| | | ○ |
| | | ○ |
| | | ○ |
| | | ○ |
| | | ○ |
| | | ○ |
| | | ○ |
| | | ○ |
| | | ○ |
| | | ○ |
| | | ○ |
| | | ○ |
| | | ○ |
| | | ○ |
| | | ○ |
| | | ○ |
| | | ○ |
| | | ○ |

| TOTAL TIME | H | M |
|---|---|---|
| 6 | | |
| 7 | | |
| 8 | | |
| 9 | | |
| 10 | | |
| 11 | | |
| 12 | | |
| 1 | | |
| 2 | | |
| 3 | | |
| 4 | | |
| 5 | | |
| 6 | | |
| 7 | | |
| 8 | | |
| 9 | | |
| 10 | | |
| 11 | | |
| 12 | | |
| 1 | | |
| 2 | | |
| 3 | | |
| 4 | | |
| 5 | | |

**COMMENT**

homepage      goseowon.com
blog          blog.naver.com/goseowongak
insta         @swk_book

인생에 뜻을 세우는데 있어
늦은 때라곤 없다.

볼드윈

**(주)서원각**

대표번호 | 02-324-2051
교재주문 | 031-923-2051
홈페이지 | www.goseowon.com
주    소 | 경기도 고양시 일산서구 덕산로 88-45(가좌동)
문    의 | 카카오톡 플러스 친구 [서원각]